W9-BON-387

SCHOLASTIC
News
Nonfiction Readers

Neptune

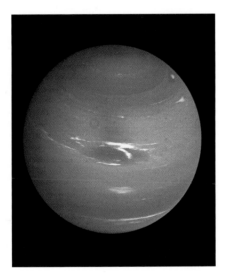

by
Melanie Chrismer

Children's Press®
A Division of Scholastic Inc.
New York Toronto London Auckland Sydney
Mexico City New Delhi Hong Kong
Danbury, Connecticut

These content vocabulary word builders
are for grades 1-2.

Consultants: Daniel D. Kelson, Ph.D.
Carnegie Observatories
Pasadena, CA
and
Andrew Fraknoi
Astronomy Department, Foothill College

Curriculum Specialist: Linda Bullock

Photo Credits:

Photographs © 2005: Corbis Images/Hulton-Deutsch Collection: 17; NASA: back cover (JPL), cover, 2, 4 top, 5 bottom right, 5 top left, 7, 11, 19, 23 right; Photo Researchers, NY: 4 bottom right, 9 (Detlev van Ravenswaay), 4 bottom left, 5 bottom left, 15 (SPL); PhotoDisc/Getty Images via SODA: 1, 23 left.

Book Design: Simonsays Design!

Library of Congress Cataloging-in-Publication Data

Chrismer, Melanie.
    Neptune / by Melanie Chrismer.
        p. cm. — (Scholastic news nonfiction readers)
    Includes bibliographical references and index.
    ISBN 0-516-24922-3 (lib. bdg.)
    1. Neptune (Planet)—Juvenile literature. I. Title. II. Series.
    QB691.C48 2005
    523.48'1—dc22

                2005002329

1 2 3 4 5 6 7 8 9 10 R 14 13 12 11 10 09 08 07 06 05

CONTENTS

WORD HUNT

Look for these words as you read. They will be in **bold**.

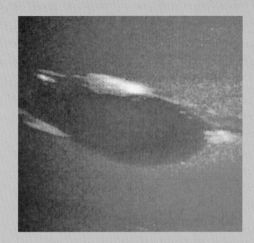

cloud
(kloud)

scientist
(**sye**-uhn-tist)

solar system
(**soh**-lur **siss**-tuhm)

4

Neptune
(**nep**-toon)

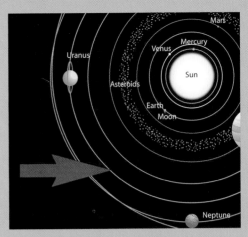

orbit
(**or**-bit)

telescope
(**tel**-uh-skope)

Uranus
(**yu**-rah-nuhss)

5

Neptune!

The planet **Neptune** looks blue.

It was named after Neptune, the Roman god of the sea.

Is there a sea of blue water on Neptune?

No. The blue color comes from the gases around the planet.

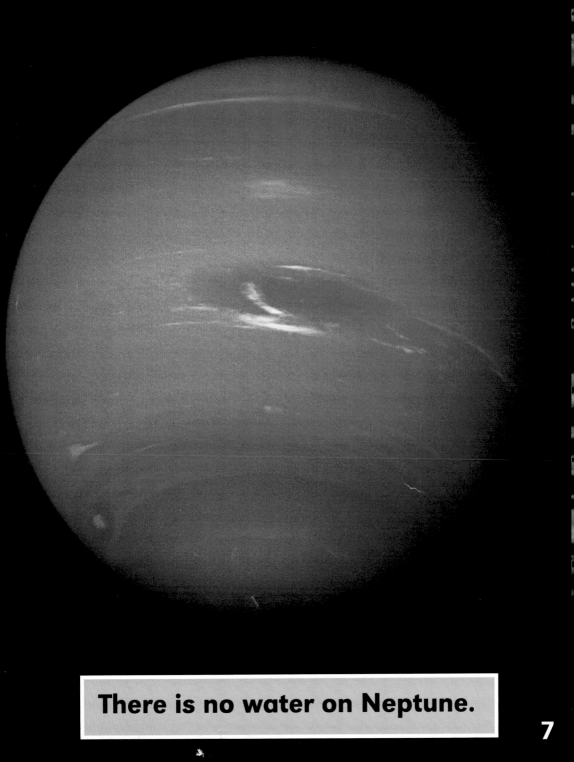

There is no water on Neptune.

Neptune is called a gas giant.

Jupiter, Saturn, and Uranus are mostly made of gas, too.

They are the biggest planets in our **solar system**.

All the planets in our solar system **orbit** around the Sun.

Neptune ➡

Uranus ➡

Saturn ➡

Jupiter ➡

Sun ⬇   **Earth** ⬅

Neptune is a big, cold, cloudy, windy planet.

It does not have **clouds** of air. It has clouds of gas.

It also has the fastest winds of all the planets.

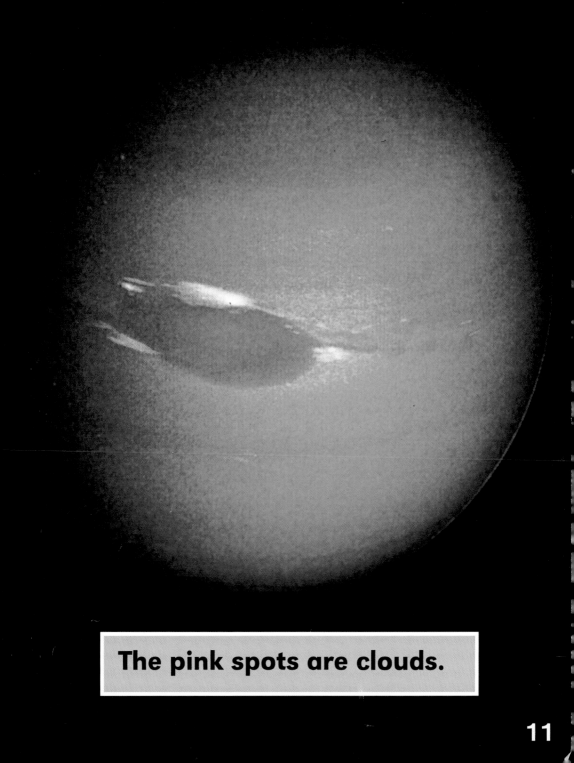

The pink spots are clouds.

Before **scientists** found Neptune they saw another planet.

This planet was **Uranus**.

Uranus wobbled as it went around the Sun.

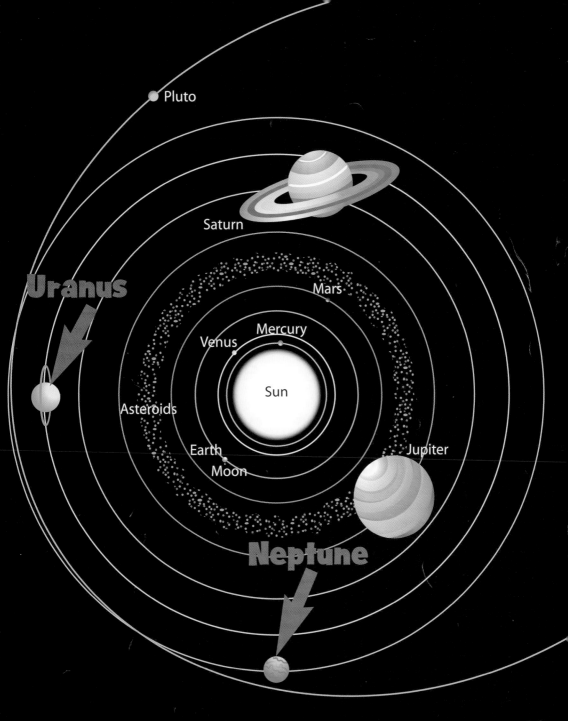

Pluto

Saturn

Uranus

Mars

Mercury

Venus

Sun

Asteroids

Earth

Moon

Jupiter

Neptune

Scientists thought the gravity of another planet was pulling Uranus.

Gravity is the pull between two objects.

Astronomers used their **telescopes** to look for the other planet.

William Herschel discovered Uranus.

Scientists used math, too.

In 1846 the astronomers found the planet they were looking for.

They named it Neptune.

John Couch Adams did the math to help discover Neptune.

Neptune was the first planet found using math.

All the other planets were found by watching the sky.

Who knows what other wonderful things will be found in space?

These pictures of Neptune were taken from the Hubble Space Telescope.

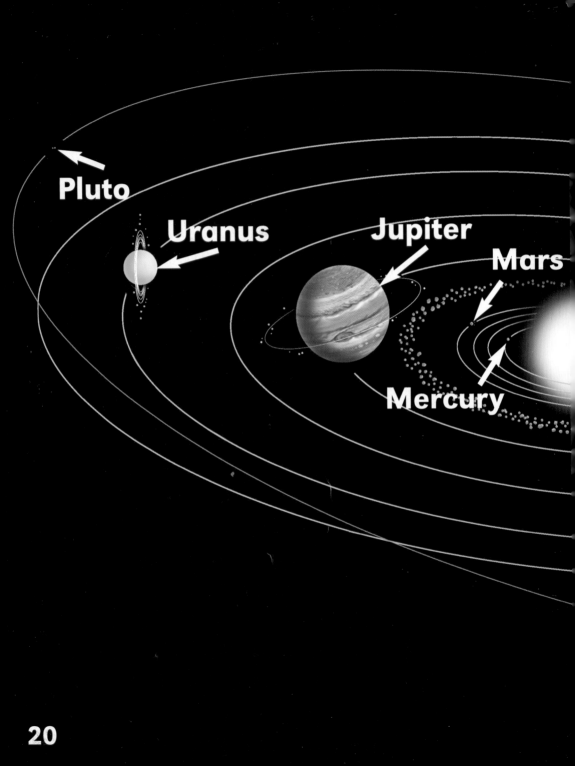

Pluto

Uranus

Jupiter

Mars

Mercury

NEPTUNE

IN OUR SOLAR SYSTEM

Sun

Venus

Saturn

Earth

Neptune

cloud (kloud) a mass that floats in the air

Neptune (**nep**-toon) a planet named after the Roman god of the sea

orbit (**or**-bit) the path around an object

scientist (**sye**-uhn-tist) a person who studies a subject by testing and observing

solar system (**soh**-lur **siss**-tuhm) the group of planets, moons, and other things that travel around the Sun

telescope (**tel**-uh-skope) a tool used to see things far away

Uranus (**yu**-rah-nuhss) the seventh planet

Earth and Neptune

A year is how long it takes a planet to go around the Sun.

 **Earth's year
=365 days**

**Neptune's year
=60,225 days
or 165 Earth years**

A day is how long it takes a planet to turn one time.

 **Earth's day
= 24 hours**

**Neptune's day
= 16 hours**

A moon is an object that circles a planet.

 **Earth has
1 moon**

**Neptune has
13 moons**

**Did you know that the
winds on Neptune can
blow over 1,200 miles
per hour ?**

INDEX

FIND OUT MORE

Book:

Next Stop Neptune: Experiencing the Solar System Alvin Jenkins, Houghton Mifflin, 2004 [full Solar System reference]

Website:

Neptune Information and Pictures
http://www.nineplanets.org/neptune.html

MEET THE AUTHOR:

Melanie Chrismer grew up near NASA in Houston, Texas. She loves math and science and has written 12 books for children. To write her books, she visited NASA where she floated in the zero-gravity trainer called the Vomit Comet. She says, "it is the best roller coaster ever!"

DATE DUE